The TODDLERS
Holiday Songbook

Stories by Heather Gemmen
Music arranged by Lynn Hodges
Illustrations by Terry Workman

Equipping Kids for Life!

www.faithkids.com

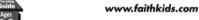

A FAITH PARENTING GUIDE IS ON PAGE 130

Faith Kids® is an imprint of Cook Communications Ministries,
Colorado Springs, Colorado 80918
Cook Communications, Paris, Ontario
Kingsway Communications, Eastbourne, England

TODDLER HOLIDAY SONGBOOK
Stories © 2001 by Cook Communications Ministries
Music arrangements © 2001 by Lynn Hodges
Cover and interior illustrations © 2001 by Cook Communications Ministries
ISBN 0-7814-3709-1

Designed by Terry Workman

First printing 2001
Printed in Canada
01 02 03 04 05   5 4 3 2 1

To Inez Unger,
adored and adoring Mother and "Mamaw" ...
... in whose loving arms and lap and heart
her grandchildren have always found
a warm and welcome refuge,
and in whose kitchen
games, stories and creative cooking projects
frequently grow into unexpected, real-life lessons
and cherished memories
Lynn Hodges

To Ollie and Willie Hiemstra:
Mom and Dad, I made this just for you. Will you hang it on the fridge?
Heather Gemmen

To my son Joshua,
You put a song in my heart every day.
Terry Workman

CONTENTS
Songs

CONTENTS
Stories

AMEN

ly-in' in a man-ger,   on Christ-mas morn- in'.

A -   men!   A -   men!

A - men! A - men! A - men! men!

1.See the ba - by,

2. See him at the seaside,
   Preachin' to the people,
   Healing all the sick ones.

3. Yes, he died to save us,
   He rose on Easter,
   Now He lives forever.

7

At Christmastime we remember Jesus as a baby.
Do you like to think of Jesus as a baby?
Do you know how special Jesus is?

At other times,
we remember Jesus
as a man.

Can you picture him at the seashore,
preaching to the people and healing the sick?

What are some other things Jesus did as a man that you like to think about?

Now we can think of Jesus in heaven watching over us. He loves us and forgives our sins.

AWAY IN A MANGER

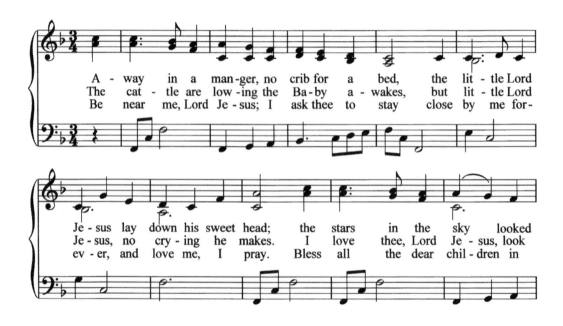

A - way in a man-ger, no crib for a bed, the lit - tle Lord
The cat - tle are low -ing the Ba - by a - wakes, but lit - tle Lord
Be near me, Lord Je - sus; I ask thee to stay close by me for-

Je - sus lay down his sweet head; the stars in the sky looked
Je - sus, no cry - ing he makes. I love thee, Lord Je - sus, look
ev - er, and love me, I pray. Bless all the dear chil - dren in

down where he lay, the lit-tle Lord Je-sus a-sleep on the hay.
down from the sky and stay by my side un-til morn-ing is nigh.
thy ten-der care, and fit us for heav-en, to live with thee there.

Away In a Manger

I like to think about baby Jesus. I wish I could have been there when he was born. I would have kissed his sweet head.

He was born in a dirty stable with animals all
around him, but everyone knew he was important.
He is God's Son and he came to earth to save us.

I am glad Jesus was born.
Christmas is a happy time.

I like to sing songs about Jesus and
I am glad he will stay by my side.

DECK THE HALL

Deck the hall with boughs of hol - ly, fa, la, la, la, la, la, la, la, la.
See the flam - ing yule be - fore us, fa, la, la, la, la, la, la, la, la.
Fast a - way the old year pass - es, fa, la. la, la, la, la, la, la, la.

'Tis the sea - son to be jol - ly, fa, la, la, la, la, la, la, la, la.
Strike the harp and join the cho - rus, fa, la, la, la, la, la, la, la, la.
Hail the new ye lads and lass - es, fa, la, la, la, la, la, la, la, la.

18

Don we now our gay ap-par-el, fa, la, la, la, la, la, la, la, la.
Sing we joy-ous all to-geth-er, fa, la, la, la, la, la, la, la, la.
Fol-low me in mer-ry mea-sure, fa la, la, la, la, la, la, la, la.

Troll the an-cient yule-tide car-ol, fa, la, la, la, la, la, la, la, la.
Heed-less of the wind and wea-ther, fa, la, la, la, la, la, la, la, la.
While I tell of yule-tide trea-sure, fa, la, la, la, la, la, la, la, la.

Deck the Hall

Everyone is singing happy songs.
Everyone is putting colorful lights on their houses.
I see huge candy canes and
pretty bells on my street.

Mommy put my presents under the tree
and a big golden star on the top.

I like eating yummy cookies
and smelling hot cider.

The whole world is having a big party
to celebrate that Jesus is born.
Fa la la la la la la la.

GO TELL IT ON THE MOUNTAIN

Go, tell it on the moun - tain, o - ver the hills and ev - ery - where;

go, tell it on the moun - tain, that Je - sus Christ is born!

While shep-herds kept their watch ing o'er si -lent flocks by night, be - rang
The shep-herds feared and trem -bled when, lo! a - bove the earth rang

24

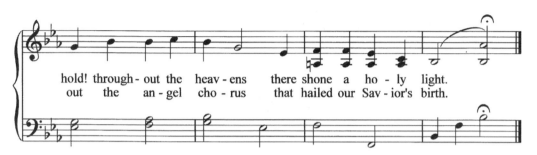

hold! through-out the heav-ens there shone a ho - ly light.
out the an-gel cho-rus that hailed our Sav-ior's birth.

Go Tell It on the Mountain

What if you were outside at night
and the whole sky lit up with angels?
I know what I would do.
I would tell everyone about it.

That's what happened
to some shepherds
who were near the place
where Jesus was born.

The angels told them that the Savior was born ...
and the shepherd told other people ...

and the other people told other people.

Nobody could stop talking about it

and now the whole world knows that
Jesus Christ is born.

JINGLE BELLS

Jingle Bells

Do you like the sound of bells ringing?
It is a happy noise.
Do you wish you could ride on a sleigh?
It would be fun to dash through the snow.

Playing in the snow is one of the blessings of Christmastime. Thank you, God, for Christmas.

JOY TO THE WORLD

Joy to the world! the Lord is come, let earth re-
He rules the world! with truth and grace, and makes the

ceive her King, let eve - ry heart pre-
na - tions prove the glo - ries of his

36

pare Him room, and heaven and na-ture sing, and_
right-eous-ness, and won-ders of his love, and_

heaven and na-ture sing, and heaven and
won-ders of his love, and and heaven won ders,

heaven and na-ture sing.
won-ders of his love.

Joy is happiness, but even better.
It is like sitting in your daddy's
lap sipping hot cocoa together
with warm bunny slippers
on your feet.

Everything is just how
it is supposed to be.

When we think about Jesus being born and being
our Lord and about the wonders of his love,
we know why the whole world has joy.

Everything is just how it is supposed to be.

LITTLE BABY JESUS

Lit-tle Ba-by Je-sus, born in Beth - le - hem;
Lit-tle Ba-by Je-sus, born in Beth - le - hem;

Lit-tle Ba-by Je-sus, born in Beth - le - hem;
Lit-tle Ba-by Je-sus, born in Beth - le - hem;

Lit-tle Ba-by Je-sus, born to be the Sav-ior of the world for
Lit-tle Ba-by Je-sus, do come in, come right in-to my heart and

you   and me;   Lit-tle Ba-by Je-sus, born in Beth - le - hem.
save me from sin   Lit-tle Ba-by Je-sus, born in Beth - le - hem.

Little Baby Jesus

At Christmastime we see many beautiful manger scenes

to help us remember that
little Baby Jesus was born in Bethlehem.

Why did Jesus become a baby? He came so that we can live forever. He came to save us.

Thank you, Baby Jesus.

O COME ALL YE FAITHFUL

O come, let us a - dore him, O come let us a -
For he a - lone is wor - thy, for he a - lone is
We'll give him all the glo - ry, we'll give him all the

dore him, O come let us a - dore him, Christ the Lord.
wor - thy, for he a-lone is wor - thy, Christ the Lord.
glo - ry, we'll give him all the glo - ry, Christ the Lord.

O Come All Ye Faithful

Jesus is God
and he became a baby.

Jesus is a mighty king
and he loves me.
Wow!

He is wonderful. He is beautiful.
He is powerful. He is almighty.

I love him and I adore him.

O COME LITTLE CHILDREN

O come, lit - tle child - ren, O come, one and all! O come to the cra - dle in Beth - le-hem's stall! And see what the Fa - ther, from high heaven a - bove, has

sent   us   to - night   as   a   proof   of   his   love.

O Come Little Children

Do you like to open Christmas presents? When someone gives you a gift they are telling you they love you.

Nothing is better than love.

Christmas is a time for presents.
Do you know why?

It's because the very best gift of all
was given to us at the first
Christmas—

wrapped in swaddling clothes
and laid in a cradle in Bethlehem's stall.

Jesus is the very best gift of love.

O LITTLE TOWN OF BETHLEHEM

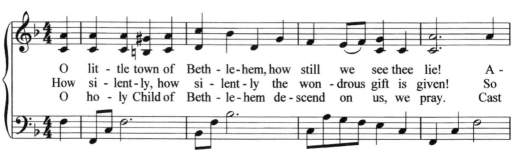

O lit - tle town of Beth - le - hem, how still we see thee lie! A -
How si - lent - ly, how si - lent - ly the won - drous gift is given! So
O ho - ly Child of Beth - le - hem de - scend on us, we pray. Cast

bove thy deep and dream-less sleep the si - lent stars go by. Yet
God im - parts to hu - man hearts the bless-ings of his heaven. No
out our sin, and en - ter in; be born in us to - day. We

in thy dark streets shin - eth the ev - er - last - ing Light; the
ear may hear his com - ing, but in this world of sin, where
hear the Christ - mas an - gels the great glad tid - ings tell. O

hopes and fears of all the years are met in thee to - night.
meek souls will re - ceive him still, the dear Christ en - ters in.
come to us, a - bide with us, our Lord, Em - man - u - el.

O Little Town of Bethlehem

When it is quiet in the house ...

and I am sitting on my bed looking out the window, I sometimes wonder about Jesus being born.

65

How did the stars know when the Child was born?

What did it sound like when the angels sang about his birth?

What did Mary and Joseph look like when they smiled down at him?

Jesus' birthday is beautiful. I love to welcome our Lord Emmanuel.

ROCKABYE, JESUS

Rock-a-bye Je- sus, my soul's fair-est treas-ure, rock-a bye Je- sus my love knows no meas-ure. Rock - a - bye Je- sus sweet, close I will hold thee, I'll hold thee, as Ma - ry's lov - ing arms

then did en - fold thee. then did en - fold thee.

Rockabye, Jesus

I like waking up early in the morning,
when everyone else is asleep,

and singing a lullaby
to baby Jesus.

71

I love Jesus

and my song is a birthday present to him.

SILENT NIGHT

Si - lent night,   ho - ly night,   all   is   calm,
Si - lent night,   ho - ly night,   shep - herds quake
Si - lent night,   ho - ly night,   Son   of   God,

all   is   bright   'round yon vir - gin moth - er and Child.
at   the   sight.   Glo - ries stream   from hea - ven a - far,
love's pure light   ra - diant beams   from Thy   ho - ly face,

Ho - ly   in - fant so   ten - der and mild,   sleep   in
heaven - ly hosts   sing   al - le - lu - ia.   Christ   the
with   the   dawn of re - deem - ing grace,   Je - sus,

74

heav - en-ly peace,   sleep in heav - en-ly peace.
Sav - ior is born!   Christ the Sav - ior is born!
Lord, at Thy birth,   Je - sus, Lord, at Thy birth.

75

Silent Night

Have you ever seen a mother holding a little baby? She gently rocks him in her arms as she looks down at her child.

She really loves him, doesn't she?

Jesus' mother Mary loved her baby too. She knew the whole world would call her blessed because Jesus would be the most special child of all.

Even the angels sang alleluia when he was born.

Fa - ther, Son and Ho - ly Ghost. A - men.

Blessings are the things that make
your life so wonderful—

like loving parents, yummy food, good friends, and fun games. All those blessings come from God. He promises to take care of us.

God gives us everything we need,

he forgives us when we
are sorry, and he helps us
make the right choices.

85

God will always be a good God

and that is why we
thank and praise him.

FOR THE BEAUTY OF THE EARTH

For the beau - ty of the earth, for the glo - ry of the skies,
For the won - der of each hour of the day and of the night,
For the joy of hu - man love, broth - er, sis - ter, par - ent child,

for the love which from our birth o - ver and a - round us lies,
hill and dale and tree and flower, sun and moon and stars of light.
friends on earth and friends a - bove, for all gen - tle thoughts and mild.

Lord of all, to thee we raise this our hymn of grate - ful praise.

For the Beauty of the Earth

Think of three things to thank God for.

Now think of three more.
Can you think of
anything else?

God has given us so
many good things,
hasn't he? We could
probably thank him
all day long.
He is the Lord of
everything but he
wants to share with us.

Thank you, God.

GOD IS SO GOOD

God is so good,
God is so good,
God is so good,
he's so good to me!

He cares for me,
he cares for me,
he cares for me,
he's so good to me!

He loves me so,
he loves me so,
he loves me so,
he's so good to me!

God Is So Good

God, sometimes when I
am singing about
how good you are and
how much you care
about me,

I want to twirl in a circle and clap my hands.

Thank you for loving me so much.

It makes me smile all day long.

FOR ALL THE BLESSINGS OF THE YEAR

For all the bless - ings of the year, for all the friends we hold so dear, for peace on earth, both far and near, we thank thee, Lord. A - men.

For All the Blessings of the Year

It is easy to say "Thank you"
when we think about how good God is to us.

Do you know that God grins a great big grin
when we sing praises to him?

I love to make God happy!
He loves to make us happy too.

Thank you, God.

Jesus was perfect. He never did anything wrong.

Sometimes I do things wrong.
It makes me feel yucky inside.

But when I pray to Jesus
and ask him to take
away all the yuck,
he does!

That's because he's perfect
and he loves me.

CHRIST AROSE

Low in the grave he lay, Je - sus my Sav - ior,
Death can - not keep his prey, Je - sus my Sav - ior,

wait - ing the com - ing day, Je - sus my Lord!
he tore the bars a - way, Je - sus my Lord!

Up from the grave he a-

rose, with a might-y tri-umph o'er his foes; he a-rose the vic-tor from the dark do-main, and he lives for-ev-er with his saints to reign. He a-rose! He a-rose! Hal-le-lu-jah! Christ a-rose!

Christ Arose

Good Friday is a very sad day.
On this day we remember that Jesus died.

It is sad to know that God punished Jesus instead of us.

But Easter is exciting.
All our sadness goes away.

Jesus Christ arose and will reign forever! Hallelujah!

GOD'S NOT DEAD

God's not dead, no he is a-live! God's not dead, no he is a-live!

God's not dead, no he is a-live! Serve him with my hands,

fol-low with my feet, love him in my heart,

know him in my life; for he's a - live in me.

119

God's Not Dead

Jesus died,
but he couldn't stay dead!

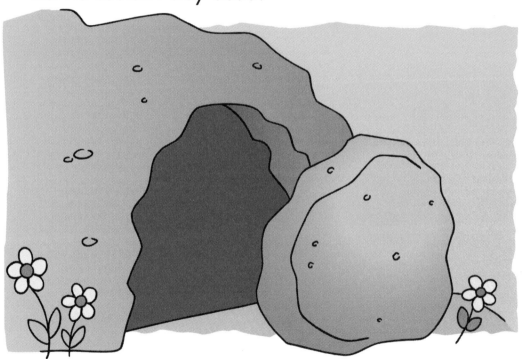

He is God.

Jesus died, but only because he wanted to save us!

He is Savior.

Yes, Jesus is alive,
I will follow him and serve him!

He is Lord.

HE IS LORD

He is Lord, he is Lord! He is ris-en from the dead and he is Lord! Ev-ery knee shall bow, ev-ery tongue con-fess that Je-sus Christ is Lord.

He Is Lord

I am so happy that Jesus rose
from the dead.
I am so happy that he
is the King.

128

I will worship him forever.
He is my Lord.

Age: 0-3

Life Issue: My children don't understand why we celebrate the holidays.

Spiritual Building Block: Faith

Learning Styles

👁 **Sight:** For a special occasion one evening, take warm popcorn into the car for your toddlers to munch on as you drive slowly through neighborhoods that display many Christmas lights. With Christmas music playing, point out all the beautiful colors and shapes of the lights to your toddlers. Let their pleasure be contagious: join in the excitement of this simple beauty. Remind your kids that Christmas festivities are all because Jesus was born.

Sound: Several weeks before Christmas or Easter or Thanksgiving, find a simple version of the biblical story. Choose a cozy place to sit and read the story to your toddlers—and make a point of coming to that spot each day to read it again. As the story becomes familiar, leave out key words for your kids to fill in and then congratulate them that they know the stories so well.

Touch: Teach your children even at this early age that holidays are not only for celebration; holidays remind us to reach out in love to others. Spend an afternoon preparing some special food to bring to another family; decorate Easter eggs and deliver them to the people at a retirement home; buy Christmas presents to give to other children. Because God has been so good to us, we want to be good to others.

Lynn Hodges is a professor of music, voice, music theory, and piano. She is the winner of numerous awards and has had multiple nominations for the Gospel Music Association's prestigious Dove Awards. She is a major partner in P&H Music, a company with an extensive portfolio of children's songs that teach life values from a biblical perspective.Lynn is married to Jimmy. They have three children: Mary-Peyton, Libby, and Nathan.

Heather Gemmen is a writer, public speaker, and editor. She lives in Colorado Springs with her husband and three children.

Terry Workman is a freelance graphic designer and illustrator. He lives in Wyoming, MI, with his wife Lisa and son Joshua.